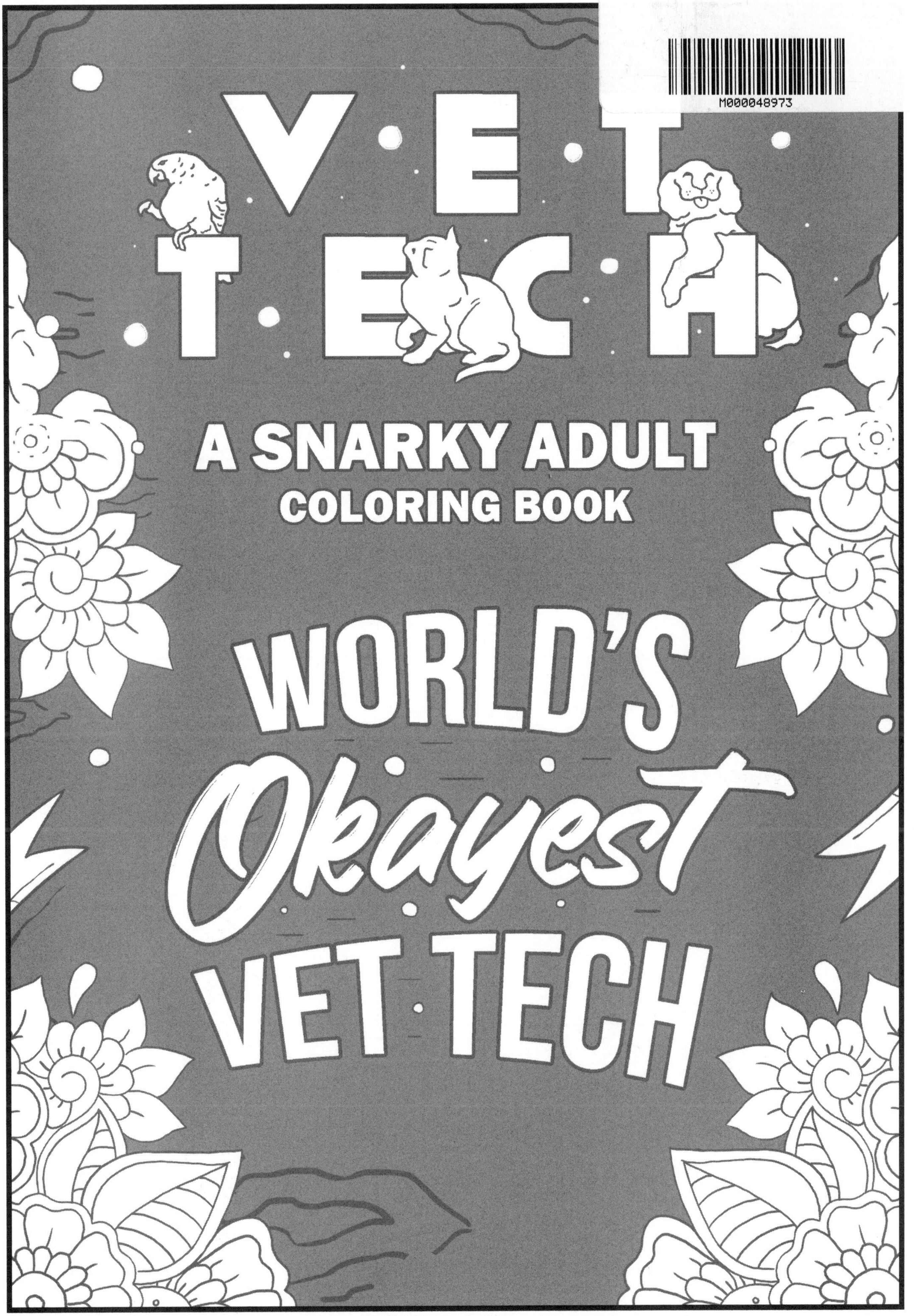
VET TECH
A SNARKY ADULT COLORING BOOK
WORLD'S Okayest VET TECH

Published By Vet Tech Passion Publishing

This Book Belongs To

____

EVERY PATIENT LEAVES A
Pawprint
ON MY HEART

I'M A
VET TECH
WHAT'S YOUR
Super
Power?

GOD MADE
Vet Techs
SO ANIMALS
CAN HAVE
Heroes
TOO

Vet Tech
BECAUSE
i can cure
CRAZY
ANiMALS
But can't fix
STUPiD
PEOPLE

NOT JUST
A Job
IT'S LOVE

Instant
VET TECH
JUST ADD
coffee

LIVE
LOVE
HEAL

VET
TECH

DON'T ARGUE
With Me
I NEUTER FOR A
Living

VET TECH
BECAUSE PEOPLE
Are Gross

WORLD'S MOST
Awesome
VET TECH

VET TECH
llama
AIN'T GOT TIME
For
YOUR DRAMA

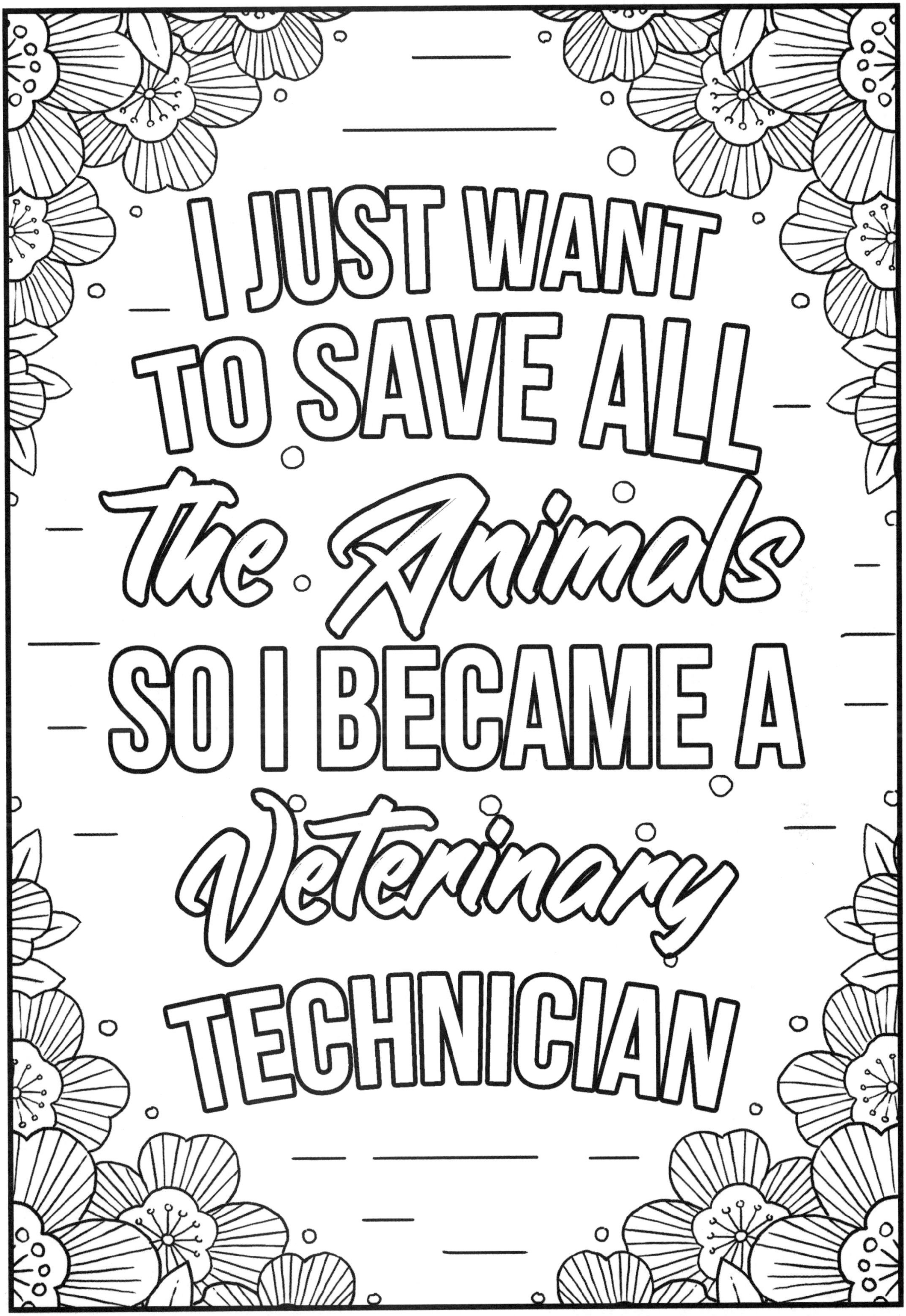
I JUST WANT
TO SAVE ALL
the Animals
SO I BECAME A
Veterinary
TECHNICIAN

WORLD'S
Okayest
VET TECH

VET TECH
SQUAD

Nurses
CARE FOR
ONE SPECIES
Vet Techs
CARE FOR
THEM ALL

LOVE

TRUST ME
I'M A
VET TECH

COVERED IN FUR
SLOBBER & SCRATCHES
JUST ANOTHER DAY
AT THE OFFICE

EAT
Sleep
VET TECH
REPEAT

Will Give
VETERINARY
ADVICE FOR
Wine

RVT

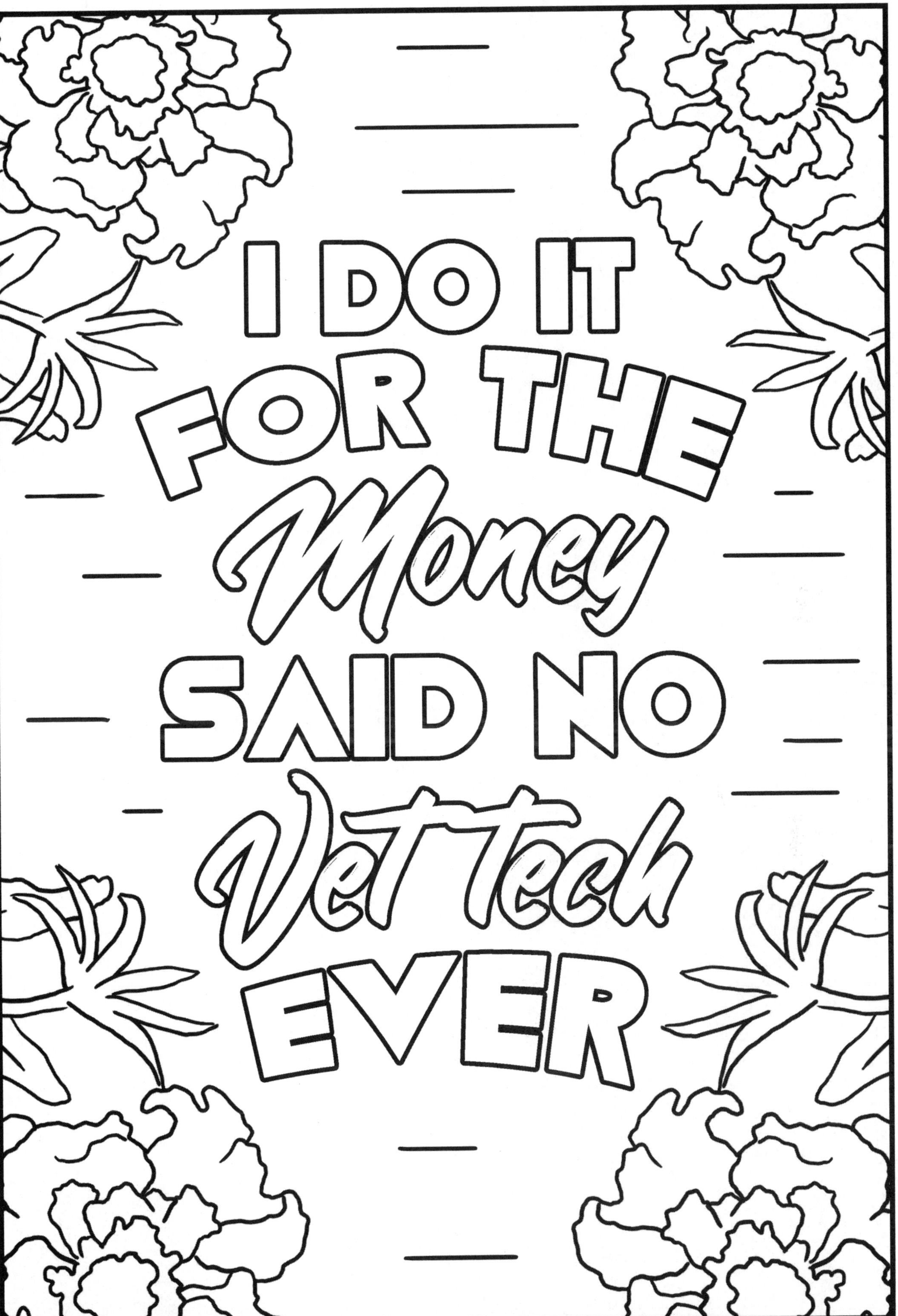
I DO IT
FOR THE
Money
SAID NO
Vet tech
EVER

SAVING
Animals
IS KIND OF
My Thing